Live Growth Focused Beginning Reader Edition

How to Excel in Life with a Growth Mindset

Dr. Michelle Ihrig

Live Growth Focused Beginning Reader Edition: How to Excel in Life with a Growth Mindset
© 2022 by Dr. Michelle Ihrig. All Rights Reserved.

Cover designed by Dr. Michelle Ihrig

Special thanks to the following envato elements designers:
aHandDrawn
betoalanis
ddraw
iconbunny
iconsoul
jumsoft
Middtone
and especially: wowomnom

Live Growth Focused
www.LiveGrowthFocused.com

Printed in the United States of America

First Printing: July 2022
Live Growth Focused

ISBN-13   978-1-946568-46-5

Dear Grown-Ups...

This book is designed to be completed in sections.

This line ⚬⚬⚬⚬⚬⚬⚬⚬⚬⚬⚬⚬ means that a new topic is going to be covered.

There are 10 themes, and all themes align across the series:
1 - Fixed Mindset vs. Growth Mindset
2 - Overcoming Setbacks
3 - School
4 - Friends
5 - Technology
6 - Teams
7 - Grown-Ups
8 - Discovering Who You Are
9 - Be True to You
10 - Being Kind

This book is written as a social story. This means that almost all the sentences include the word "I." If your child struggles in a particular area, you can continue to revisit the theme. Then help your child learn the sentence, and then role-play the scenario.

For example, if your child struggles with being kind, when your child is calm, revisit the page "I will be kind to others."

Ask your child what is means to "be kind." If they can't think of anything, then help them.

Ask them what are times when someone is not kind. Make sure that the unkind moment you are addressing is included... perhaps not sharing, pinching someone, or throwing things.

Now, go back to what it means to be kind and how can they show kindness to others. Spend a few moments with them practicing being kind.

End by saying, the next time (struggling situation) happens, what will you do?

"I will be kind to others."

Practice/role play the scenario one more time.

Then, give them high-fives/hugs and let them know you are proud of them.

If a situation arises when they begin to demonstrate the unkind behavior, get to their eye-level and remind them in a calm voice...

"Remember what we practiced? I will be kind to others. Are you being kind?"

The longer that you can stay calm and remind them of what you taught them, the better.

You might need to adapt this method based on age...though consistency will work. 😊

I dedicate
this book
to my
students.

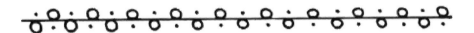

Growth Mindset:

Always do your best

even when it is hard.

I am going to learn about

growth mindset.

A growth mindset means always
trying my best.

I will do my best in music
and art.

I will do my best in science
and sports.

I will be a good thinker.

A person with a fixed mindset does not like to try.

A person with a growth mindset loves to try.

Fixed Mindset Faces

Growth Mindset Faces

7

I can choose to have a growth mindset.

Life can be hard at times.

Sometimes, I feel sad, angry, or upset.

I will learn
from my
mistakes.

I will think about happier

times...

like eating
ice cream,

going

swimming,

playing music,

or building with Legos.

When I learn, I grow.

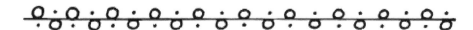

Sometimes,
I like to learn new
things.

Sometimes,
I like to play
instead.

Sometimes,
I like to use the
computer.

Sometimes, I like
to read instead.

Asking questions helps me
to learn.

My brain works hard when
I learn.

Growth mindset means doing my best, even if it is hard.

Making new friends

is a good thing.

Sometimes, I like to paint with my friends.

Sometimes, my friends want to do something else instead.

I am a good friend

when I take turns.

Someone might make me feel sad.

I will tell a grown-up when I feel sad.

I will be a good friend.

Some kids spend too much time
using technology.

When adults were younger,
things were different.

Adults did other activities
without technology:

like reading,

skating,

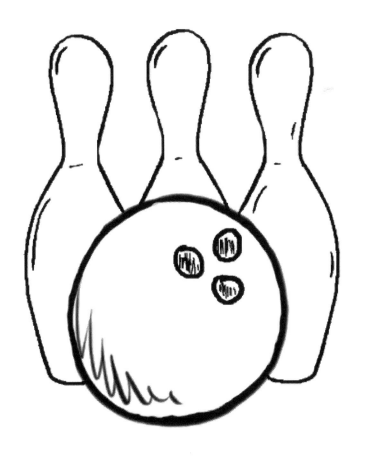

or bowling.

Be careful not to use
too much technology.

I will balance my time.

I will help my brain grow.

I will make good choices about technology.

A team is a group
of people who do the same
thing together.

Some people are

on swim teams.

Some people

are

on baseball

teams.

When I am on a team,
sometimes I talk, and
sometimes
I listen.

I am always kind and fair.

I help my teammates
be their best.

Growth mindset is about helping others be their best.

Grown-ups help me learn.

I learn how
to play games.

I learn about the outdoors.

When I help at home,
I am being kind.

Sometimes,
I help
in the
kitchen.

Sometimes, I help
put clothes away.

I can talk to a grown-up
whenever I need help.

Helping others is a good thing.

I like to play
with trains.

I like to
listen to
stories.

44

I like to go to school.

It is okay to like different things.

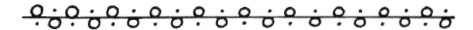

Sometimes, I like
to paint.

Sometimes, my friends want to
do something else.

Sometimes, I like to go to the playground.

Sometimes, my friends like to
listen to music instead.

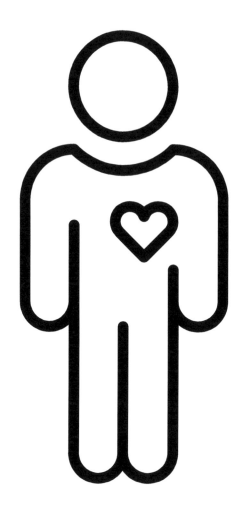

It is okay to want to do
something different.

50

I will learn how to do new things.

 I will be kind to others.

I will listen to my family.

I will be peaceful when I talk.

I will tell the truth.

I will ask questions.

I will learn new things.

I will say "I am sorry" when I make a mistake.

I will say "I forgive you," when someone apologizes.

I will help the world to be a
better place.

I will be loving and kind.

I will use a growth mindset.

Doodle Page

Doodle Page

Doodle Page

Doodle Page

Doodle Page

Doodle Page

About the Author

Dr. Michelle Ihrig is an author/educator based in Atlanta, Georgia. Her passion is inspiring others. She believes: When people believe in themselves, they are unstoppable. Dreams become obtainable, Success is fathomable, and Hope abounds.

Dr. Ihrig is a certified educator in Mathematics, Special Education, English as an Additional Language, Gifted Education, Online Education, and Administration. Her doctoral focus was on best practices of inclusive education at international schools.

Dr. Ihrig is also the author of Scripture Life Devotionals and Black Bear Coloring Literacy Books - all available on Amazon.